THE HAZARDS
OF HOLINESS

THE HAZARDS OF HOLINESS
THE CROOKED LINES OF GOD

THE HAZARDS
OF HOLINESS

POEMS 1957–1960

by Brother Antoninus

DOUBLEDAY & COMPANY, INC.
GARDEN CITY, NEW YORK

8 11
A 63 L

Cum Permissu Superiorum

L

The author wishes to express his gratitude to the following publications in which some of these poems were first published: *Big Table #2, Jubilee, Damascus Road, Chicago Review, The Critic* for "All the Way to Heaven," Copyright © 1962 by The Thomas More Association; *Chicago Choice* for "I Am Long Weaned," Copyright © 1962 by The Poetry Seminar, Inc.; *Ramparts* for "The Hazards of Holiness," Copyright © 1962 by The Layman's Press; *Atlantic Monthly* for "The Song the Body Dreamed," Copyright © 1962 by Atlantic Monthly Co. Lines from "The Three Voices of Poetry" by T. S. Eliot, which appeared in *On Poetry and Poets,* are reprinted with the permission of Farrar, Straus & Cudahy, Inc.

Library of Congress Catalog Card Number 62–15940
Copyright © 1958, 1959, 1960, 1961, 1962 by Brother Antoninus
All Rights Reserved
Printed in the United States of America

FOREWORD

We gaze at such men in awe, because we gaze not at a work of art, but at the re-creation of the man through that art, the birth of a new species of man, and, it may even seem that the hairs of our head stand up, because that birth, that re-creation is from terror. . . . They and their sort alone earn contemplation, for it is only when the intellect has wrought the whole of life to drama, to crisis, that we may live for contemplation, and yet keep our intensity.

—WILLIAM BUTLER YEATS
The Trembling of the Veil

In the foreword to *The Crooked Lines of God* I spoke of the aridity which gradually tightened upon my spirit in the first years of my religious life, shutting off the creative flow. When I began to write again it was perhaps inevitable that this subject itself should become the matter of my poems. T. S. Eliot, in his essay "The Three Voices of Poetry" speaks of the poet as one

oppressed by a burden which he must bring to birth in order to obtain relief. Or, to change the figure of speech, he is haunted by a demon, a demon against which he feels powerless, because in its first manifestation it has no face, no name, nothing; and the words, the poem he makes, are a kind of exorcism of this demon. In other words again, he is going to all that trouble, not to communicate with anyone, but to gain relief from acute discomfort; and when the words are finally arranged in the right way—or in what he comes to accept as the best possible arrangement he can find—he may experience a moment of appeasement, of absolution and of something very near to annihilation, which is itself indescribable.

This objectification of inner experience becomes the most efficacious of all acts of relief, except prayer. The underblows of the mind have their own laws, the reverse of all the pilgrim had been taught to expect; for though in the first part of his journey the direction ran straight enough, from bad to good, from dark to light—in the extremity of the onward search and the exhaustion

—5

of its intense luminary symbolism, the other side of the personality, darkly inscrutable, rises into consciousness, like a kind of nightfall that overtakes the traveler before his time, and imposes upon him the threatening figures of its antithetical disproportion. These have now to be faced and assimilated, and it is the facing out that immobilizes the wanderer with its undercast of fascination, and its overcast of dread.

These poems, then, are all poems of that famous Dark Night of the Soul, which has become so commonplace in literary reference as to seem, by this time, triteness itself—except to those who undergo it. For its reality, unequivocal, and outside the dispersion of any superficial literary effect, registers itself too powerfully in the quest to ever be dismissed. Against the grain, compounded of the hallucinatory and the obscene, no less than of the transcendental and the sublime, the imagery seeks back against the primordial anguishes, encounters the mute demon and the vocal ghost; that Prince of Darkness himself, who, most appallingly, is yet named Lucifer, presence of light—he it is who stands at last between the soul and its God. Yet on this very exigence turns the dreadful crux: if Lucifer hides behind man, does God, then, hide behind Lucifer? Many a mystic, many a saint, has mistaken the devil for Christ, Christ for the devil. And if such as these have blanched in the encounter, what hope for the poet, with his extravagant imagination and his friable nerves? These are the terrible wrestlings his verse begins to register; and this is the harrowing ambiguity, so fraught with terror and mystery and meaning, that cross-riddles this demon-haunted realm.

These things are obvious in the poetry itself. I speak of them only in order to explain what might seem singularly offensive to some, might seem, indeed, blasphemous to others. Believe me, this is not so. If I encounter in them the demon (and I do) I also experience as well that deliverance which Eliot salutes, which was my whole impetus of quest. There are those who find the very attempt irrelevant. A critic once spoke of my failure to transmute my feelings into real poems: "a process which he understands, I think unfortunately, not as a victory over language, but over himself." It is perhaps one sign of my maturation that this judgment, which was so painful for me to receive at that time, I now recognize as being quite true; and I am in fact serene in it.

This is not to say that I despise craftsmanship, but only that the struggle with language is the struggle to make myself comprehensible to myself, to orient my inner and outer being. As Claudel says, "Every word is the expression of a psychological state, caused by attention to an outside object." Between the "heresy of expressive form" (shapelessness) and the "heresy of *a priori* correct form" (rigidity) one gropes toward the ineluctable authority of synthetic form, in which all relevant elements are synthesized into an indefinable whole. I say indefinable because only that which possesses mystery can manifest the character of wholeness. A poem, like a dream, is "whole" to the extent that it registers the mystery of the psychic complex which produced it. My poem can never be "perfect" because I cannot be. If I ever achieve a "victory over language" it can only be partial, and only to the extent that I have achieved a "victory over myself."

Thus I can truthfully say that I have no interest in the conquest of language, as understood by those who seek to achieve a hypostatized aesthetic object. The victories I seek, those of "appeasement, and absolution, and something very near to annihilation," are one and all victories over myself, the unremitting attempt to exorcise the demon. My poems are trophies, scalps torn dripping from the skulls of interior adversaries, seized in the blind grapple of the encounter, to bring back to the civilized consciousness as witnesses that I did keep faith. Or rather, if it is not presumptuous to so speak, they are veils, like Veronica's, that took the smutch of the bloody visage when the Spirit collapsed under its cross.

For it does collapse, time and again. I have been writing poetry for thirty years, and despite my failures, I have known this encounter, this appeasement and absolution many times, but only momently. More and more, as the inner core clarifies, as the uses of poetry grope toward the most obscure reductions of the inner being and descend into the darkness below, I see what I felt most dimly from the beginning: such expirations, for all their momentary apotheosis, are all anticipatory, they lack finality. These dizzying cancellations, lunging between the defeats of language and the victories of self, are all Stations of the universal Cross, in whose temporal achievement it is not given to rest.

For there is one death to be earned, a martyrdom beyond the most grandiose formulations of the conceptual mind, with its masochistic engrossment and its ludicrous falsification of the real; and I crave and fear it with a rapacity and a terror I never believed possible. In its realization all the disparate attributes of the self, and all its irrelevances, will suck into the Absolute on which everything is gauged, and I will grope down to it, as the wader moves by instinct into torrents insuperable to the mind, and is swept away. That death is God. It will come to me, correct the errors, liberate the imperative evocations, cancel the admonitions, and all the gangling stumps of truncated endeavor—those victories, my failures, which I seized up and love.

For I know that within me the Christ stirs and straightens, steeling the soul to achieve a victory no poem can celebrate, no demon deny. Let all these scalp locks stiffen with my blood, I am done with them. I have torn them off, and nailed them exultantly up, and even knelt before them in blind idolatry, but that is over. In the museums of the future perhaps they will be curiously reclaimed, exhibited to the imaginations of those who have never known the pain, and who count it an interesting curiosity to ponder the barbarisms of a sanguinary past. That would be false. For even then, even as they gaze, out in the darkness men more sensitive and complex than any now living will be wrestling the demons of their own deliverance, draining their heart's blood to their knees, and the zone of that Death on their faces.

BROTHER ANTONINUS

St. Albert's College
Dominican House of Studies
Oakland, California
November 24, 1960
Feast of St. John of the Cross

CONTENTS

I — FRIENDSHIP AND ENMITY

JACOB AND THE ANGEL

*And Jacob was left alone; and there wrestled a man with him until
the breaking of the day. And when he saw that he prevailed not
against him, he touched the hollow of his thigh; and the hollow
of Jacob's thigh was out of joint, as he wrestled with him. And
he said, "Let me go, for the day breaketh." And he said, "I will not
let thee go, except thou bless me."*

—THE BOOK OF GENESIS

I dream I am on a caravan traveling to the Holy Land, except that
I seem also to be an exile coming home at last. We are on camels
with Arabs in charge. At nightfall we come to a deep stream and
make camp, expecting to cross over the next morning. I go to sleep
among the beasts and dream that I am finally approaching my
father's house; our old dog comes running out to meet me, but when
I go inside, the house is deathly vacant. I wake up fearful in the
night; a weak moon has risen and the caravan is gone. I rush down
to the water and start to cross over, but an obscure figure on the
opposite bank defends it with a rifle. I realize that the Arabs are
thieves, that this is a loyal servant guarding the ford against their
depredations. I realize too that my association with them has cor-
rupted me, so that I am indistinguishable from them, and that
they have used me to gain their ends, which is my guilt. The
Defender is crouched behind a bush when he sees me start over.
He rises up straight as a hunter, tall as an avenging angel, his gun
level, his aim deadly. I wait for the bullet to strike. It seems to be
coming from a tremendous distance, like some meteor from outer
space, plunging timelessly toward earth. In the eon of its flight I
feel within me the whole destiny of the human race in its struggle
toward realization, with all its hopes, ecstasies, sins and conflicts
incredibly concretized within my one tormented life-span, and
actualized in my very flesh, as if I were its sole issue. The water
closes over my head, but I cannot believe that this is the end. I
make toward the Defender a gesture of desperate truth, to somehow establish the authentic character of what is real, to assert its
indestructibility over against the wastage that is washing everything away. I do not know if he hears me. My act of attestation
becomes my act of final consciousness, delivered in a reach of tremendous affirmation toward his presence there on the bank. I have
no sense of success in this effort, but as I go down it is as if the very
extremity has somehow purged and transformed the energies within
me, endowing there a core of absolute existence, which is pure, and
over which, I know, the waters can have no final power.

—— *13*

His mother's fondness wrought his father's frown.
Supplanter from the beginning, struggler in the womb,
Heel-holder, the overreaching scion. She egged him on.
For her offense she saw him hounded out of home
Nor lived to look again, ever, on the longed face.

Well warned if rudely, weaned, the outflying son
Beheld the laddered angels in their intercourse with earth,
His first liberating sign, if late. In that deliverance,
Freed from the mother's death-hug, trended east,
And over the well-dark water gazed on the sudden bride.

But guilt had split him. Deep down the offended father
Lived on symbolic in the maid's evasive sire,
His mother's brother. Duped by the blear-eyed sister
In his bed, trickster out-tricked, he swallowed gall,
And suffered the serfdom of those sweat-compounded years.

Suffered and loved and prospered. Even in bondage
His talents stood him well: the slat-eyed ewes
Bred neatly, flocks flourished, his wealth was won.
Seizing his sunk soul force he broke for the border;
Faced out the father on the slope of Galaad.

Faced, forced the offender, and sudden victor, saw
The signifying angels at the Camps of God,
Mark of the second liberation. Father-freed,
He gathered up the measure of his mind, turned home
To offer restitution, expunge the ancient debt.

But fear still fouled him. The raw unreckonable guilt
Sapped at his manhood, guttered his whole-felt strength.
Off there the beaten brother mustered up his men.
How could the exile know but that the wound
Had sown a poison, wrathful, had festered the sullen years?

And falling on his face he prayed to God, and rose
Dividing family from family, setting flock from flock,
Over the ford of Jaboc. Shivering he watched them
Breast the dark water. All was committed now. Alone
He waded the freshet last in the apophatic night.

But hold. Tall by the boulder, athwart the torrential flow
Spied out one shadow menacing that ford.
Esau? Stalking perhaps the hazardous creek-cross,
To there assail the pilgrim in his pass,
Bash out his brains, usurp his anguish-garnered hoard?

Fear! Fear! Midstream the exile wavers,
Tortured by guilt, doubt-wrung, his guts all gone.
About his loins the death-dragged water seethes,
Creeling his doom, and the grainy flints of fate
Sift and suck out beneath his terror-fastened feet.

No help. No hope. Nothing. If this be Esau
Then Jacob meets his star. Brother to brother,
Shadow to lipless shadow, the twin identities
Confront. Deep down his spirit gropes. Desperate
He grapples that stranger in one fierce convulsive rush.

This, then, at last, the divine engagement.
Who wrestled with his brother in the womb
Wrests now the angel. The years go down tumultuous
Beneath his trampling feet. O mother-favored son
What deed of truth did all those phantasies prefix?

One queasy crime—and the score-long exiled years!
How many mockeries of the inscrutable archetypes
Must we endure to meet our integration?
Is it fate or merely malice that has made
Us overreach our brother in the burdened womb?

Is it fate or merely malice that entraps
Us early in our own self-hugging hearts,
Darlings of our mother's doting eye, to steal
The kindly blinded father's foremost blessing,
Too soon seize up the giddy promises of God?

Fatality or malice, either-or, that curse
Curses us cold. We in our sin will never see
The glad, long-looked-for land. Mother-duped exiles,
Skewered on our father's guilt, we learn, we learn
Too late to face the angel, engage the hidden God.

All night they fought. All night the home-starved son
Turned in torment in the angel's withering grasp,
There on the trampled weeds by the root-grown shore
Where the sullen winter freshet, flushed with grit,
Rushed by like passion in the black prophetic night.

What vast eternities hang here contained?
What conflicts down the long genetic line
Suffer their extirpation in the wrestler's stance?
High overhead the great globed constellations
Hover like circling birds above the struggled heads.

And far down the planet's dark nocturnal side
The night-wombed nations murmur into birth.
His sistered wives, confused and terrified,
Twin aspects of his dark divided life,
Crouch in the weltering night and moan for his reprieve.

Dogged the man fights on, grappled wrist and knee,
And when the dawn blurs in the time-pressed angel
Glances at the east and makes to go.
But the exile, obdurate, closed in the unremitting
Grasp, exacts the specific blessing that he needs.

The man has won. Standing at last alone
He staggers on the twisted thew, if not
Invincible at least undaunted. This anguish
In the sinew is his sign, his final liberation,
Seal of the smiling God, the serene benediction.

Hurt but truly healed he sways, who seized
In the heart's black hole the angel of intellection,
And rose renewed, in the soul's great upsurge shaped.
His painful deprivations all converge
To make the anguished synthesis of his perfection.

And is called Israel, striver with God, and limps
Into the light of the huge ingesting sun, and meets
The long-feared brother: who beholds a saint,
Measured in the furious siege of grace, and seeing
Weeps on that placid neck, kisses the God-calmed face.

ALL THE WAY TO HEAVEN

All the way to heaven is heaven.

—St. Catherine of Siena

And the Lord said to Satan: Behold, he is in thy hand.

—The Book of Job

All the way to heaven
Is Hell. And the devil posts it.
Prince of this world, devourer of souls,
Whose mandate keeps the very inches of our lives
In specious fee, we trudge, we trudge, stumble year-long,
Limp through the ancient shires of our affliction,
Tormented . . .

Dust of the earth
Is all we have to walk with
And the dust is his.

Dust of the earth
Stacked to the mortal frame.

Dust, and the dust is his,
Given him, his private use,
His plaything, his horrible
Doll.

Man walks: a demon
Smirks, crouches
On his shoulder,
Clots his ear.

Man sleeps: a demon
Hulks, debouches
In his brain,
Reeling the motion picture of his dream
From mad to vile.

Man loves: a demon
Sulks, slouches
In his heart,
Kindling a winy rancor . . .

Love strips, lascivious.

Oh, brother-devil!
Shadow and adversary!
My keeper!
Double of the heart's imago!
I do acknowledge!
I do concede!

Your virtuosity
Confounds my virtue.

Your foresight
Botches my insight.

Your prescience
Tortures my sentience.

Dabble your fretful finger in my blood, Hellhound!

I bear thy obscene vision in my breast
And tread thy mill with staves upon my neck!

A SIEGE OF SILENCE

A siege of silence? Thy meaning-moving voice
Hushed in the heart's crypt, thine eye
Shut in unreckoning slumber—
God? God? What storms of the dredgèd deep
Your absence lets, the rock-croppage mind,
Kelp-girthed, sunken under swell,
All seas of the unislanded soul
Typhooned, hurricaned to hell!

God! God! A place of eels and octopuses
Opens down under! Hell-stench
Sulphurs the waters, the drench of madness
Gags my plunged head! Death's belly rips!
The Devil's ruptured fundament,
Fawning with reechy kisses,
Strokes my lips!

God, to purge the memory pure
What cautery is needful?
To ease the soul of rancor,
Quench its hate?
God, God of the paradisal heart
I wait!

PASSION WEEK

Christ-cut: the cedar
Bleeds where I gashed it.

Lance wound under the narrow rib.

Eve's orifice: the agony of Abel
Enacted out on the Tree.

Blood gushed
From the gash.

Tho Holy Chost
Gusted out of the sky
Aghast.

Our Guest.

Bleed cedar.
Little cedar,
Lanced,
Axe-opened,
The ache of sacrifice.

Pour out,
As Christ,
Those pearls of pain,
Bequeathed.

O bleed
Little cedar,
Bleed for the blooded Heart,
For the pang of man . . .

The earth's
Old ache.

ZONE OF DEATH

Wind is not nigh.

No Holy Ghost,
Spirit outspilt,
Burnt this charred day.

What sin did this?
Could I?

Hot light blares.
Stars, outblistered now,
Mark time, extinct.

Night might bring
The seasonal constellations
In its sphere,
But night is nowhere.

Sun. Sand.
The noon-crazy jays
Cackle and gibber,
Jar on the gritted ear.

Dawn sneaked in unsmelt.
No wine, no water here.

Now the lance-riddled man
On yon pronged tree,
Stretched in the death-tread there,
Opens his executing eye
And gibbets me.

WHAT BIRDS WERE THERE

Wheresoever the body is, thither will the eagles be gathered together.

—SAINT LUKE'S GOSPEL

I dream that I am leaving the scene of an execution. Night has fallen, and I am walking slowly through deserted country. The execution has been awesome rather than terrifying, and as I meditate on what has happened, it is as if I can see about me, in the night-shapes of bushes, the dark figures of various great birds, which, as I pass between them, settle into the contours of human heads. I become aware that these are the faces of the executioners, hardening as they transform into abstract and hieratic projections, without personality, serving to represent fixation points of human nature, utterly inflexible in their particular constellations of consciousness, and I know they will never relent. I think how sad it is that nature cannot reject the logic of its own determinism. Then I come out upon a clearing, and notice on my left a hill of graves, and an owl, like that of Minerva, perched upon a stone. Looking west I see the moon, with the face of a diseased woman, sinking into the sea.

Two magpies under the cypresses.
And what birds were there then I wonder,
To make a graveness in the afternoon
When the nailing was done to the cross hilt,
The man-act centered on the heart of God, irrevocable?
Sparrows, to be sure, scratching about in the street offal,
Yes, curb-brawlers, common as fleas,
Picking right and left for barley seed in the horse manure.
Doubtless a meadowlark off on a fence,
V-breasted, his splendor-drenched throat
Reaved on the spontaneous uprush
Of a rapture unremarked.
Or perhaps that treetop dandy the oriole,
Spinner of gestures, withdrawn now deep in his solitary covert,
His dulcet song, like rich contralto,
Unnoticed on that air.

Say rather, and more to the point,
Two gyrfalcons for outriders sweeping the cross quarter,
Circling, kleeing their strict sabbatical cries,
Imprecational and severe as executioners,
A curse on all triflers. Say further,
The mountain raven, malevolent prophet,
Utterer of virulent indictive oaths,
Imperious from the lodgepole pine,
Damnation drawn down out of the black beak inexorable.
Say too the appalled roadrunner,
Off in a fright scandalized over the stubble patch,
The town curs yelping after. Say most significantly
That grim gliding keeper of appointments, that dark
Ceremonial purist the vulture, a frown on the sky,
Methodical as an undertaker, adaptative
And deferential as the old woman of griefs
Who wraps up the dead.

But this does not mean, small birds of a feather,
That you, in your earnest beneficent presences,
Were somehow inapposite: linnets and speckled finches,
Fleet swallows, sheer swifts of the chimney;
Nor may it impeach your own most consonant
Purling evocative condolence, rain doves of the roof.
Better than those who thumbed sharp iron and plaited thorn!
Better than those who rattled dice for a stranger's shirt
And sponged galled water! Better than those
Who palmed hard silver to close a deal and slunk off after,
Too guilty to haggle! Oh, better by far
Than any of these were you, were you, flit messengers,
Arrived at that place all unbeknownst of what was toward,
But quietly there, not come but *sent*, keeping a tryst
After friend and foe had all alike gone over the hill,
Back down to man's dearth, man's glib and man's madness,
Nor left any light, the owl only upon the slab

To mourn the ruse when the moon sagged out, exhausted,
Her face demented, her jaw half gone,
Till the fierce star of morning
Pierced like the inner eye of God that scorning cloud,
Birthmarked that dawn!

II — THE DARK FACE OF GOD

SAINTS

*Amen, amen, I say to thee: when thou wast younger, thou didst
gird thyself and didst walk where thou wouldst. But when thou
shalt be old thou shalt stretch forth thy hands, and another shall
gird thee, and lead thee whither thou wouldst not.*

—SAINT JOHN'S GOSPEL

I dream I am on pilgrimage to Rome. My group is taken into the
catacombs and we see the labyrinthine tunnels branching out here
and there into the earth. I wander away and find myself absolutely
alone. Suddenly I come upon a coffin—not an ancient specimen, as
one would expect to find in such a place, but strangely out of
context, like something from the nineteenth century—the coffin, say,
of St. Thérèse of Lisieux, or St. Bernadette. In fact I am reminded
of the famous photograph of St. Bernadette clothed in her bridal
gown and laid to rest in her coffin, which has always seemed to
me to epitomize the immolation of the feminine sensibility. In my
dream I kneel beside this strange coffin, but when I look inside I
discover it to be quite empty. This is more disquieting to me than
if I had beheld a corpse, and I start up in alarm. Off in the reaches
of the labyrinth I hear the slow drip of water, terrible, like time
running out.

I who ravished a joy lost under my hand
The very rapine killing it.
Who stole for profit
What vanished that moment
I made it my own.
Who murdered for fear
What murdered me,
Its violence breaking out of my fist,
That suicide, my rape.

Man's heart!
What improbable depths are delivered up
When the seizure of faith grips the soul-string,
Bitted, heels it head over,

The long light thrown where darkness has dreamed
On untouchable snakes in their birth-nests,
Fosters the worm that gnaws on ever,
The unkillable core . . .

Man's heart!
To have known it indeed:
Confused, sensitive, cunning, depraved—
Most glorious!

God made it;
Man ruins it.
God-in-man wright in purity and defilement
What neither alone could ever make be!

Not even God
Has power to force an evil act
But man does!

Every day he does!

I do!
Every day I do!

That work between us, God and I!
He the maker and I the destroyer!
Tearing down what he builds,
Besmirching what he pondered pure,
Profaning what he sanctifies!

O man!
Spirit screaming in the flesh!
Flesh screaming in the spirit!

Saints!
What secrets do you hold,
Pursed in your mummified lips,
Inscrutable back of the stiffly smile?

We thousands questing kneel here,
Beseech, our lips
Mumbling on invocation,
Twisting the rosaries of our supplication,
Knuckled hands, this desperateness,
These hope-dazed eyes!

You know!
We know you know!
You lived it through!
Fought up-ramp to the battlement,
Grasped the fell fiend on the pike-sill,
Rattled him till his teeth broke,
Flung him down all yowling into the dark descent,
Smashed all bloody damn him on the rocks below!

Yes?
Did you not so?
Was it not so done
When you did it,
Saints?

Saints!
Born out of sinners,
Sinners reborn!
In sanctity beatified—
That is all sainthood means,
Is it not,
Saints?

Your dead lips
Stretch on a secret
Not even you
May ever reveal.

Souls and warriors!
Great-hearted ones!
How may we hope to learn of you,
Of anyone,
For a course of battle
That can't be seen
Ever at all?
When what is relatable
Broke at a level beyond any ken?

Even you, even you,
Never really knew it, saints.
Stalwarts of the soul's war,
Prechosen.

But woke one morning
Dead and glorified,
Nobody more surprised than yourselves.

And looked back doubtless
As some thorn-torn climber
Pants at the peak-top,
Staring down in amaze
At the hell of cockle
He clambered through.

I've done that.
Looked back down all choked and bleeding
At what I crawled across,
Raking scorpions and poison-mouthed toads
Off my clothes as I stared.
I know that.

But now ahead
No cactus there nor any beasts,
No toads, no snakes,
No devils and no ghosts.

Nothing.

No thing. Not anything.

Not to be named, even,
Cursed at, grinned back against,
Invoked, knelt to,
Adored, denied, befouled or hated!

And nothing to love!

A blankness
Like neither night nor day
Confronts: the flat void
Of unrealization.

Before what will be
Is.

Before what might be
Can.

Like music you realize exists
But never hear.
Like terror you know alarms
But do not fear.
Like hope you know lives on
But can't conceive.

O soul!
O vast potentiality unprobed!
Be touched! Be opened!
Be moved! Be crushed!

God, withholding being
Just out of grasp,
Do something!
Kiss or kill
But move me!

Make me! Slake me! Back me! Break me!

A labyrinthine maze
That has no walls nor floor
Prevents.
A sea that has no wave nor depth
Foments.
A water without wet
Torments.
A life without a death
Dements.

God? Saints? Faith? Rapture? Vision? Dreams?—
Where?

I place my hand out.
Lead me!

I step, thus.
Lead me!

Lead me!

YOU, GOD

A land of darkness, and of the shadow of death, without any order, where the light is as darkness.

—THE BOOK OF JOB

Nor any day gone,
Nor any night,
Measureless over the rimrock.

Nor those black imaginary suns
Roaring under the earth,
Roasting the roots of trees.

If I beg death, God, it is of you.
If I seize life, it is out of you.
If I lose, if I lose,
It is into you.

God of death,
Great God of no-life,
Existence is mine,
But you
Broach a nothingness
Breached out of nowhere.

Always you are not yet.

Deep in my guts,
Choked on oblivion,
Split, hearted on annihilation,
Caught through,
Smothered out,
A terror of emptiness,
Spat.

Immutable silence
Enormous over the snow mesa,
Enormous over the lava crag,
The wind-worked cloud.

My brain
Burns on your pierce.
My blood splits.
I shriek each nerve.

God!

Suck me in!

A FROST LAY WHITE ON CALIFORNIA

Thou shalt not offer the hire of a strumpet, nor the price of a dog, in the house of the Lord thy God, whatsoever it be that thou hast vowed: because both these are an abomination to the Lord thy God.

—THE BOOK OF DEUTERONOMY

Once again I dream I am on pilgrimage, walking alone through dark woods, far from human habitation. As I enter a clearing I am startled by a slight movement to one side, and see a little dog cowering beside a corpse, watching me with beseeching eyes. Drawing near I perceive the body to be that of a woman, huddled under a cloak, with one white arm extended. The arm takes on a powerful erotic significance, almost magical in the quality of the dream, so that I instinctively pull back; but the piteous whimper of the dog compels me, and bending down I gently roll the body over, exposing the face of the victim. The blood from the mouth is jaggedly striking in a stagy, melodramatic way, as in the silent films of my boyhood; and indeed the woman is very beautiful in the unreal fashion of those heroines. Then I see bruises on her throat signifying strangulation. I intuit instantly that this has been a rape, and drawing back the cloak I see the skirt still wadded awkwardly above the hips. She is lying on her side, and from between the compressed thighs trickles the dried bloodmark of defloration. I hastily cover her again, and straighten the poor, sprawled limbs, but under the cloak they nevertheless seem to lie almost wantonly in death. The flesh is still pliant, although from the dog's starved look I believe he has been on guard here a good three days. I wonder if this pliancy is miraculous, like that of certain deceased saints, and with this thought a suffused light begins to radiate from the countenance of the murdered girl. Suddenly I am unaccountably grief-stricken, and kneeling beside the corpse, sobbing, I clasp it to my breast, as some precious object now irretrievably lost. The head rolls back, exposing the beautiful throat to my gaze, and the terrible, strangely familiar bruises of the hands. At this moment I hear across my shoulder a cynical male voice. "Go ahead and cry," it says inflexibly. "That's just the way she looked when I raped her." Suddenly my sobs sound hollow and forced, like discreet coughing. I realize with a certain flintlike insensibility, more villainous than any outburst of passion, that of course the voice is my own.

God. Spell dawns
Drained of all light.
Spell the masterhood of the means,
The flanges of extinction.
Spell the impotence of the numbed mouth,
Hurt, clenched on the bone of repudiation,
Spurning.

I grind it down. I grind on it.
I have yet to eat it up.

Crouched in my choir stall,
My heart fisted on stubborn revolt,
My two arms crossed on my chest,
Braced there, the cloak
Swaddling me round.

It is night.
I bore the darkness with my eyes,
Tearing it up.

Over the chapel the cold
Snaps on the roof,
Ringing with silence.
Two hours, spanning two inches of darkness.
I feel stars like hoarfrost prickle the tallness.
There ought to be a dawn.

"Do you think, O man, in that high
Toss of desire, that sheer
Aspirative hanker of yours,
What deeps go unplumbed?
Something within you is grinding its axle,
Spitting out sparks.

Stop for one moment,
Or ever so little,
And be assured you have read it aright.
That which is written between those flanges,
Spelled on the walls of the vascular heart,
Is your own scrawl.
What scars have you gouged on the stone of that cave?"

Fingered down in my deeps, I deny it.
What desolation, that depth!
Who says so!
What secret, that scrivening!
My own business, you.
Leave me alone.

"Do you think," cried God, "to have spat in my face
Driving me off that easily?
I ask you nothing not accorded a dog:
One glance of recognition.
To own what I am.
Which is you.
I am your image!"

The dark held through.
The stars, frozen, spit seeds in the sky.
I thought giant Orion,
The club-tossed arm,
Hurls over the house.
At ground level the frost
Gnawed at, bit tree-trash,
Loose leaf-stuff.

"I will not quit you," cried God, "for we are inseparable!
Do you hear? My name
Is carved in your heart,
There among the graffiti,

In capital letters.
That is my gash,
The struck brand,
The wound you made in your violence.
It will never heal.
You do not know how much I am you:
The other side of your face,
The back side of your body.
I stand between your shoulders.
I am that void behind your eyes
When you can't think!"

I wondered about the dawn, where it could be.
I sensed the wind veer south and west.
Two days it had held
To die in that quarter.
And in such death, out of that clear, frost fell.
Now the choir
Hung black and empty,
Hell's belly.
I felt the new wind, south,
Grope her tonguing mouth on the wall.
What does she want, this woman-wind?
She is trying to rain.

"Never forget," cried God, "I am your slave!
Call me and I come.
Curse me, I cannot quit.
I have never renounced.
Do you know what I am?
I am your woman.
That is my mouth you feel on your heart,
Breathing there, warming it.
I am more. I am your dog.
That is my moan you hear in your blood,

The ache of the dog for the master.
I am your dog-woman.
I grieve a man down,
Moan till he melts."

There was a rustling of winter-scarred weeds in the gutter.
It was winter, midwinter.
It was night, midnight, past midnight.
It was the dawn night. The scars in my heart
Were gashed by a terrible hand.
I clenched my heart on that gash.
I cursed.

"You are of flesh," cried God, "that is your light!
The shimmering sensitivity of the nerve.
Not I!
No brain to think with!
No nerve to think through!
I am dog in that I follow,
Woman in that I love.
Seek me!
In the heart of your disgust,
The germ of your revulsion,
The glint of truth impacted in your terror.
Invade me!
Flee that Luciferian
Light of the brain,
Pride of your life!
Down! Down! Behind! Below!
Quick! I am gone!
I, woman, moan against the bars.
I, dog, bay against the dawn."

I raised my head.
On such a night, long ago, when I was a boy,
There would have been a rooster

To rip the silence with a murderous yell.
I heard the wind turn west, southwest.
I said to myself: Do you think it will rain?

"Do you want it to," cried God, "and what for?
This ground is frozen.
Frost has locked hard on it now for too long.
The seeds are all tight.
Their lips are sealed.
They wonder when it will come a change.
They are like you."

I jerked back my hood,
Fighting the ache of my bones.
I am a fool.
Birds stirred out there in the crotches of bushes.
What red-breasted linnet will throat that dawn,
His voice a thorn?

"I have nothing to conceal," cried God, "from those deeps of your
       passion!
Why should I lie?
Read your own hate if you would know.
Would I squander blood on such as you if I didn't mean it?
Bah! I am always in earnest.
My hunger is plain as the pang in your gut.
Feed me! I am you!"

Was this a dream,
Some phantasy of anguish?
I crouched in my stall all night.
It was winter, midwinter.
A frost lay white on California.
I felt stars crack blue in my brain.

"I ask nothing of you," cried God, "that you wouldn't accord a
    dog!
I told you that!
The sheerest recognition.
That I do exist.
That I am yours.
Close your eyes now and be *what I am.*
Which is—yourself!
The you *who am I!"*

The roof of the chapel split up the sky,
A tree-wedge in a stump.
I felt the cold stitch my bones.
I should be in bed.
This is a fool to knock about here in the frozen hour,
Champing my teeth like a chittering ghost.
Who do I think I am?

"*Who, indeed,*" cried God, "*when you think what you think?*
Ask me who, I will tell it!
How far do I have to go?
Look! I crawl at your feet!
I, the God-dog!
I am all woman!
I eat from your hand!
Feed me. All I ask is your heart.
Am I that ugly?"

The light woke in the windows.
One by one the saints existed,
The swords of their martyrdom healed in their hands.
The linnet opened his voice;
He blistered his throat on the seethe of that rapture.
The suddenness split my skull.

"No pride!" cried God, "kick me I come back!
Spit on me I eat your spittle!
I crawl on my belly!
What is revulsion to me?
As free of disgust as of shame and pride.
As much your dog as I am your God.
Whatever you need.
When you have gutted this madness
Drop down on the ground.
I will lick your hand."

That was the moment the dawn dragged in,
The cloud closed. It had slid from the sea,
Almost a sneak. I stood up in my stall,
Flung off my cloak. I heard the rain begin.

It was falling on the roof,
A slow spilth of deliverance,
Falling far, very far.

It was falling, I knew, out of the terrifying helplessness of God.

Into the frost,
Into the frozen crotches of the bush,
Into the feather of the singing bird.

Across the stuttering mouths of those seeds;
Against the sob of my tongue.

I AM LONG WEANED

> *When I looked for good then evil came, and when I waited for*
> *light then came darkness. My bowels boil, and rest not.*
>
> —THE BOOK OF JOB

I am long weaned.

My mouth, puckered on gall,
Sucks dry curd.

My thoughts, those sterile watercourses
Scarring a desert.

My throat is lean meat.
In my belly no substance is,
Nor water moves.

My gut goes down
A straight drop to my groin.

My cod is withered string,
My seed, two flints in a sack.

Some day, in some other place,
Will come a rain;
Will come water out of deep wells,
Will come melons sweet from the vine.

I will know God.

Sophia, deep wisdom,
The splendid unquenchable fount:

Unbind those breasts.

IN THE BREACH

God!

The I-killer!
The me-death!

Rip me out!

Crouched in my womb,
Reality-butting head,
Mute-mouthed,
Gagged.

Breach!

Head-hunched,
Pelvis-pulled,
Heel-seized,
Sky-swung.

God!

My first scream
Skewers all night.
Far down
Earth's groan,
Gripe-gout,
The mother-grunt,
Gasps.

Where I?

God!

Caul-freed
I cry!

46 —

SLEEP-TOSSED I LIE

Sleep-tossed I lie,
Midnight stemmed under,
And the bloat moon
Shut in its sky.

Lord, Lord of these tangled sheets!
My wrestling's witnesses
Certify my heat.

I have lain long, lain long,
Long in thy grasp am lain,
Lord of the midnight watchings,
The monk's tongue-shuttered groan
And the hermit's heart-ripped cry.

Somewhere the wanton lovers keep
Vigils of fecklessness,
Their hearts
Bursted on passion
And the body's blade
Plunged deep.

And in that death find sleep.

But I? Long have I lain,
Long lain, and in the longing
Fry.

Sleep-smooth this brow.
Bless with thy rippling breath
These anguish-awkward limbs.

Grant thy surcease.
Toy me no more, Lord.
Lord of the midnight wrestlings
Keep the peace!

THE WORD

One deepness,
That mammoth inchoation,
Nothingness freighted on its term of void,
Oblivion abandoned to its selflessness,
Aching for a clue.

What clue?

Syllabled,
Shaken in its fixèd trance,
A far shuddering.

Who?

Blooms,
Subsumed in its quality
Of inflection.

Endowed,
The syllable focusing,
Determination conceives.

The concept
Borns of its pure consistency.

Not willed but perceived,
Not declared but acknowledged,
Yielded into the dimensional,
A salutation from the without.

Bearing within it strange liberties,
Consanguinations,
Dissolutions of oldness.

Rarer than the splendor it invokes,
More of wonder than its focal
Justness of perfection.

BLACK CHRIST

The day of the Lord is darkness, and not light. As if a man did flee from a lion and a bear met him; or went into his house, and leaned his hand on a wall, and a serpent bit him. Shall not the day of the Lord be darkness, and not light? Even very dark, and no brightness in it?

—THE BOOK OF AMOS

I dream that I am at my mother's funeral in the Masonic Temple in Selma. Her body is in the coffin, and yet it is I who am of her body—in this dream I am my mother's spirit. Her sister-members of the Eastern Star have completed the Masonic rites and go past me weeping like sorrowful wraiths. I understand their temporal involvement in pain, grief, guilt and reaction, but I am no longer of it, and have little interest in it. I can see the newly dug grave in the cemetery, out beyond the city limits. The earth is black, very rich, potent, supremely fertile. It possesses a subsumed, immaterial reality, like a vital presence. I lie in a state of expectation. It is as if my psychic life has the power to persist in time after the body's death, the pseudo-death. But that grave and that earth are Death itself, the real death, creative death. I lie abstractly aware of the muffled commotion about me, the family huddled suppressed and confused, painfully inarticulate, trying numbly to adjust to the fact that I am gone. I alone am not confused—all stillness, quietude, and expectation, a bride awaiting her marriage, this Death. The disturbances seem to go on and on, useless, meaningless involvement. Soon I will be received, merged in the marriage, a swift absentation from the world, and only this has significance. At last they start to roll me out. Beyond the doors: bright sun, the broad steps descending, a sea of faces, the massed automobiles, the open hearse. But I have awareness only for that single place, that Hole—straight, severe, black, deep—off beyond the roofs and the city limits, which fastens me with a cumulative possession as I am borne toward it, leaving as I pass from this shimmering world and the marmoreal hallucination of time, only the exhalation of my soft divesting sigh.

Heart not cry
Nor mouth moan?

——51

I dread life,
The illusion.

I stand in life,
In light,
And woo death,
Dis-illusionment.

I dare not die,
Knowing not.

But I woo death,
Though I know not,
Know nothing.

Undeceive me, God.

Death is not ours,
We ourselves do not die:
Are killed.

Only you, O God, deliver.

Craving the cancellation
To possess the clarity,
I crave the truth
Beyond the illusion,
This nonexistence.

Let me exist,
Die unto the totality,
Half dead now
Of the nonexistent.

God, who can neither
Deceive nor be deceived
Is darkness,
My death.

Lucifer, who forever
Deceives and is deceived,
Is light,
My life.

Dark God, dark
God of death,
Thou art good—

Then *be* good,
Release.

Kill me.

Relieve me of the weight,
Relinquish me into the dearness,
Thyself,
That depth.

Redeem me into existence,
That darkness,
Thy love.

I beg thy kindness,
That dark
Unrapture.

Kill me.

I beg the lowliness
Of thy love,
That depth.

I beg thy kindness.

Merciful darkness,
The strict sweetness of terror.

Impeccable lovely fear,
The divine revulsion.

Holy unspeakable horror,
Beautiful annihilating pain.

The splendid and terrible anguishes,
The sublime insuperable hurts.

These the disenchanters,
Angels of deliverance,
Radiant sisters of mercy,
In their dread hands
Is borne the peace.

Send them, Lord.

Make me a marriage,
Death, my master, my Christ.
Keep thy bed holy,
My cross.

Kill me.

My body, thy cross,
Make pregnant with thy seed,
Swell into definition,
Stalk of thy desire.

Black bridegroom,
Dear and dreadful Christ,
Deliverer,
Possess me.

Giddy I live.

Unable to die,
Drunk of the illusion,
The ruttish wine,
Lurching with deceit,
Unfit . . .

Giddy, I live on.

III — LOVE AND VIOLENCE

A CANTICLE TO THE GREAT MOTHER OF GOD

> *Now all good things came to me together with her, and innumerable riches through her hands, and I rejoiced in all these; for this wisdom went before me, and I knew not that she was the mother of them all. Which I have learned without guile, and communicate without envy, and her riches I hide not.*
>
> —THE BOOK OF WISDOM

I dream I am on a hill overlooking San Francisco. I stand to the east across the bay, the light falling forward out of the west and north as it does toward sunset in summer. I see the merging lines of traffic, usually reminiscent of scurrying ant trails, but now transforming into processions, perhaps religious processions in solemn chant intent upon the source of their life and vitality, slowly descending from the long bridges and the winding freeways beneath me, out of the latency of the darkening world behind. At last I see the outline of the city recede, until in its place only a sublime presence persists, a mysterious feminine implication, evocative and potent, like the memory of the Beloved, evading definition or the strictness of analysis, but haunting and omnipresent. Across the void of that awareness one gull, white-bodied and agile, wheels toward the sinking sun. In the coming of the night, touched by a perfect peace, I stand a long time until, far out in the Pacific, the light drops, and on the darkened west the crescent moon emerges. Then I go down, but neither the crash of traffic, nor the threat of whatever predatory violence menaces the slums through which I wander, can dispel from my mind the reality of that moment, which persists, like a permanent bestowal, and which, I cannot doubt, will change my life forever.

Sometimes I dream you measured of bright walls, stepped on
    a hill and diademed with rose,
Sea-cinctured, the black wave-haunted wharves radialed round
    your hems, and the nuzzling tugs
Shunted like suckling spaniels at your piers.

All the resplendent bridges of your bays converge upon your
    heart to there deploy,

Dilated into streets, fanned to the outmost sectors, bloodlines of
    pulsant use that throbbing flow,
Serving the induct of all crafts and hallowed skills.

Trending into your colonnades at dawn, down from those air-
    girthed arches of the sky,
We pause in tremble, sleep-cozened but reprieved, stirred to the
    richening diastole.
Soaring on noon we sense it loudly replete, swelled to the stately
    tempo, augmented to the day-drummed dance,
Pace of the proudness, an opulence subsumed, the strident fluting
    and the resonance of blare.
Sinking toward dusk we drink a slowed, more moded music,
    muted, a hushed convergence, a deep relapsed repose.
In all the hinterlands about the trains come nosing home, mal-
    lowed of late light,
Shrilling their long crescendos, creaming with racing lamps the
    fast ingathered gloom.
Night is your nuance. Listening we hear the wild seabirds, flit-
    tered like intuition through your coolest thought,
Falter and then fly on, seeding steep sky, the beacon-raftered
    verge,
South-sought, mewling one plaintive meed, a tremulance of
    plight, before they pass,
Reflashing on pale tips the birth-reverted instinct of all trek.

Hidden within the furlongs of those deeps, your fiery virtue im-
    pregnates the sky, irradiant with wisdom.
You are Byzantium, domed awesomeness, the golden-ruddy rich-
    ness of rare climes, great masterwork of God.
Kneeling within thy moskey naves, seized in the luminous indult
    of those dusks,
We hold the modal increase, subsumed in chant, ransomed of the
    balsam and the myrrh.

Keeping an immost essence, an invitational letting that never
    wholly spends, but solemnly recedes,
You pause, you hover, virtue indemnable, at last made still, a
    synthesis unprobed.
Checked there, we tremble on the brink, we dream the venue of
    those everlapsing deeps.

But always there is a somethingness eludes us, Mother, city and
    citadel,
Proud battlement and spire, croft, granary, and the cool, sky-
    thirsting towers.
Obscure behind those nodes, those many-mingled lights, that
    wink and then well up,
Pale opals on the movement of your breasts, or the navel-cuspèd
    moonstone at your womb,
Always your essence hovers. The flashing glances of the sea belt
    you about with brightness, blind our eyes,
And the famished senses swoon of that vaunted spicery.

For how could we ever know you wholly as you are, thou who
    are clearly here so manifest of God?
Our coarseness keeps us pinioned of our nerves, while you, im-
    maculate, conceived simplicity,
Subsume the inviolable instance. We are unworth, who shunt in
    stupor whelming at your breasts,
Rude shoulderers who sully what we seek, foul our sole good.

But you, that which you have, you give, and give it graced, not
    as it is but as we use it of you,
Dimensioned down to our foreboded taste, our thirst of need,
    filtered to our mereness and our plight.
We suck through sin. Our boon is that you are subsistent of the
    light, bringing the Light to us, whose darkness dams out
    grace.

Confirmed unto the kindness, gaped mouths of thirst, we tongue a
    milk like honey,
And know from whence it sprung, being yours, who never could
    taste the heaven-nurtured nectar that you use.

Believe us when we seek, Mother and Mercy, who in our lives are
    unbelievable,
All faithlessness of the flesh wrought flaccid, the stunt will
    burdened in the bone.
That need we nurse is sharper than our cry.
Through you alone, the Wisdom and the Womb, keen-creeps the
    child,
The visionary life fast-set against the acrid element, death's
    factual zone.

Clearly you are to us as God, who bring God to us.
Not otherwise than of those arms does grace emerge, blessing our
    birth-blank brow.
Wombed of earth's wildness, flank darked and void, we have
    been healed in light,
Traced to the sweet mutation of those hands, a touch closing the
    anguish-actual stripe,
Whip-flashed the sin, lip-festered on our soul.

This is all plain. But plainness drowns in everything you are, the
    presence you proclaim,
That mystery in which achieves all you are meant.
Squinting our eyes we cannot comprehend.
You we behold, but never what makes you be, the Allness you
    relate to,
The Finalness you keep, and which we ache to touch.
This thing neither can you say, because of us, lacking your whole
    capacity to know.

But see: out of this too redounds your deepest motherhood;
As one unable to yield the child that utterness no child can spell,

She yet *subsumes* the truth, *is* the grave wisdom of her wakeful
    eyes.
Or else the child, callow-stumped and closed, never grows up to
    what deep knowledge is, completes its mode.
Our spirits, watchful, tenacious on their term, see to it only as
    it gleams in you, because of what you are,
The radiance on which the world's blunt might is closed, sharp
    in a singleness simple as any star,
Bright-bought, sheer as one nexus-seeding coal.

Hive of the honey, city and citadel, cathedral and cloister and the
    cool conventual keeps,
Receive us in. The anchorhold of heaven helms us on.
Hungered of that pledge we trample up the ramps limned of a
    vision,
Questing for what you smile of veiled in rapture mirrored in your
    eyes,
A solace deeper you said than all such clustered balms,
Pierced to a presence totaled on all truth, vaster than the
    prophet's dream descried,
And larger, if we believe you, even than your love.

IN ALL THESE ACTS

Cleave the wood and thou shalt find Me, lift the rock and I am there!

—THE GOSPEL ACCORDING TO THOMAS

Dawn cried out: the brutal voice of a bird
Flattened the seaglaze. Treading that surf
Hunch-headed fishers toed small agates,
Their delicate legs, iridescent, stilting the ripples.
Suddenly the cloud closed. They heard big wind
Boom back on the cliff, crunch timber over along the ridge.
They shook up their wings, crying; terror flustered their pinions.
Then hemlock, tall, torn by the roots, went crazily down,
The staggering gyrations of splintered kindling.
Flung out of bracken, fleet mule deer bolted;
But the great elk, caught midway between two scissoring logs,
Arched belly-up and died, the snapped spine
Half torn out of his peeled back, his hind legs
Jerking that gasped convulsion, the kick of spasmed life,
Paunch plowed open, purple entrails
Disgorged from the basketwork ribs
Erupting out, splashed sideways, wrapping him,
Gouted in blood, flecked with the brittle sliver of bone.
Frenzied, the terrible head
Thrashed off its antlered fuzz in that rubble
And then fell still, the great tongue
That had bugled in rut, calling the cow-elk up from the glades,
Thrust agonized out, the maimed member
Bloodily stiff in the stone-smashed teeth . . .

                                          Far down below,
The mountain torrent, that once having started
Could never be stopped, scooped up that avalanchial wrack
And strung it along, a riddle of bubble and littered duff

Spun down its thread. At the gorged river mouth
The sea plunged violently in, gasping its potholes,
Sucked and panted, answering itself in its spume.
The river, spent at last, beating driftwood up and down
In a frenzy of capitulation, pumped out its life,
Destroying itself in the mother sea,
There where the mammoth sea-grown salmon
Lurk immemorial, roe in their hulls, about to begin.
They will beat that barbarous beauty out
On those high-stacked shallows, those headwater claims,
Back where they were born. Along that upward-racing trek
Time springs through all its loops and flanges,
The many-faced splendor and the music of the leaf,
The copulation of beasts and the watery laughter of drakes,
Too few the grave witnesses, the wakeful, vengeful beauty,
Devolving itself of its whole constraint,
Erupting as it goes.

In all these acts
Christ crouches and seethes, pitched forward
On the crucifying stroke, juvescent, that will spring Him
Out of the germ, out of the belly of the dying buck,
Out of the father-phallus and the torn-up root.
These are the modes of His forth-showing,
His serene agonization. In the clicking teeth of otters
Over and over He dies and is born,
Shaping the weasel's jaw in His leap
And the staggering rush of the bass.

GOD GERMED IN RAW GRANITE

God germed in raw granite, source-glimpsed in stone?
Or imaged out in the black-flamed
Onyx-open line, smoldered in the tortured
Free-flow of lava, the igneous
Instant of conception? As maiden-form
Swells in the heaviness of wold, sleeps
Rumped and wanton-bulged in the boulder's
Bulk, is shaped in tree-forms everywhere
As any may see: dropped logs, say, or those crotched
Trunks pronged like a reckless nymph
Head-plunged into the earth—so Godhood
Wakes under water, shape-lurked, or grave and somber,
Where sea falls, mocks through flung foam . . .

                                        Ghost!
Can this be? Breather of elemental truths,
She stirs, she coaxes! Out of my heart's howk,
Out of my soul's wild wrath
I make oath! In my emptiness
These arms gall for her, bride's mouth,
Spent-breathed in laughter, or that night's
First unblushing revealment, the flexed
Probity of the flesh, the hymen-hilted troth,
We closed, we clung on it, the stroked
And clangorous rapture!

                I am dazed.
Is this she? Woman within!
Can this be? Do we, His images, float
Time-spun on that vaster drag
His timelessness evokes?
In the blind heart's core, when we,
Well-wedded merge, by Him

Twained into one and solved there,
Are these still three? Are three
So oned, in the full-forthing
(Heart's reft, the spirit's great
Unreckonable grope, and God's
Devouring splendor in the stroke) are we—
This all, this utterness, this terrible
Total truth—indubitably He?

THE SONG THE BODY DREAMED IN THE SPIRIT'S MAD BEHEST

I am black but beautiful, O ye daughters of Jerusalem. Look not upon me because I am black, because the Sun has looked upon me.

—THE CANTICLE OF CANTICLES

The Imagination, unable to grasp the reality of pure Spirit, conceives of their union under the modality of her own nature. Longing to respond totally to the divine summons, and convinced in faith that the Redemption has rendered this possible, she struggles to cast off all the inhibitions of original sin, and evokes the deepest resources of her sensuality, in order to achieve in shamelessness the wholeness of being an age of shame has rendered incomplete.

Call Him the Lover and call me the Bride.
Lapsing upon the couch of His repose
I heard the elemental waters rise,
Divide and close.

I heard Him tremble and I turned my head.
Behold, the pitiless fondness in His eyes;
Dark, the rapacious terror of the heart
In orgy cries.

His eyes upon me wanton into life
What has slept long and never known the surge;
Bequeath an excess spilt of the blood's delight,
And the heart's purge.

His lips have garnished fruits out of my breast
That maddens Him to forage on my throat,
Moan against my dread the finite pang
Of the soul's gloat.

He is the Spirit but I am the Flesh.
Out of my body must He be reborn,
Soul from the sundered soul, Creation's gout
In the world's bourn.

Mounted between the thermals of my thighs
Hawklike He hovers surging at the sun,
And feathers me a frenzy ringed around
That deep drunk tongue.

The Seal is broken and the Blood is gushed.
He does not check but boldens in His pace.
The fierce mouth has beaked out both my eyes,
And signed my face.

His tidal strength within me shores and brunts,
The ooze of oil, the slaver of the bitch,
The bull's gore, the stallion's famished gnash,
And the snake's itch.

Grit of great rivers boasting to the sea,
Geysers in spume, islands that leveled lie,
One snow-peak agonized against the bleak
Inviolate sky.

Folding Him in the chaos of my loins
I pierce through armies tossed upon my breast,
Envelop in love's tidal dredge of faith
His huge unrest.

But drifting into depth that what might cease
May be prolonged until a night is lost,
We starve the splendor lapsing in the loins,
Curb its great cost.

Mouthless we grope for meaning in that void
That melds between us from our listening blood,
While passion throbs the chopped cacophony
Of our strange good.

Proving what instinct sobs of total quest
When shapeless thunder stretches into life,
And the Spirit, bleeding, rears to overreach
The buttocks' strife.

That will be how we lose what we have gained,
The incremental rapture at the core,
Spleened of the belly's thick placental wrath,
And the seed's roar.

Born and reborn we will be groped, be clenched
On ecstasies that shudder toward crude birth,
When His great Godhead peels its stripping strength
In my red earth.

THE HAZARDS OF HOLINESS

I. THE BEHEADING OF JOHN THE BAPTIST

> *And when the daughter of the same Herodias had come in, and*
> *had danced, and had pleased Herod and them that were at table*
> *with him, the king said to the damsel: "Ask of me what thou wilt,*
> *and I will give it thee."*
>
> —THE GOSPEL OF ST MARK

John cried out—the excoriate definition
Of the invincibly sane. Naked adultery
And the greed of caste lolled notorious
In the royal sheets. The true tongue damned it.
Herodias, that corrosive female wrath,
Black grasp of the invidious breed,
Blanched, swore blooded reprisal.
But the Tetrarch, sensitive, winnowing those careful
Cross-fertilizing fears, that tease of the politic heart,
Smelled dangerous fire in the prophet's blood,
Checked his hand. Dungeoned deep, a claw of conscience
Repressed in the brutal heart of the State,
The Baptist dreamed implacably on,
Manacled but unmaimed.

                    Salome danced.
Night of the tentative April moon,
A great guest-gathering, the air
Stung out of torrents and the freeze of caves.
She danced through the great encircling fires,
Among the lounging electrified troops.
This the Machaerus, steep fortress,
Stained with the gullied blood of invasion
And the howling native pang. Below: oblivion,
The salt-festered sink of the Dead Sea,

Sodom's crusted containment. She danced, pubescent,
In the heart's early ungovernable rage,
The fateful foot now perilously in quest,
Sentient of in indued splendor,
Path of the mortal wound.

"Give me the head
Of John the Baptist!" cried the violent girl,
Her eyes like an eaglet's blazing behind her unbrooched hair,
Mouth insolent with wine, throat panting
Those covetous gouts that howk toward murder,
The dauntless breast beating that oath up out of her blood,
Her sovereign demand. "On a plate! On a plate!"
She turned, imperious, her legs spread like a man's,
One naked arm distended, the savage bracelets
Aclash on her wrist. The Tetrarch, hooked,
Brooded momently over his cup of death.
Truly this grieved him. Looking plaintively round
He smiled, squirmed, lifted the hand of lifeless assent,
Concurred. Axe-chopped, the sublime features,
That had stared down priests and the brutality of queens,
Rolled in the mire, a girl's wild wish.
She had danced, had she not? Twirling her loose skirt,
The nubile thighs flashing the ringlets of excitation,
Flamboyant, the inflammable gestures of a crude sexuality
Nascently alive, a virgin gambling away her maidenhood
In the crouched animality of arrested stupration,
That thrust of blood in the heart's valves when treasure is spewed,
The toothed heels stuttering out a mirthless crescendo,
Rapacity unflexed, the impossible strut of childish excess,
Astute circlings of consanguinity, most ancient of inversions,
Blood calling to the blood.

Clash the spears, warriors!
Throw down those drinking goblets onto the stones,
You sunburned fighters, swart treaders of Asia,

Dirk-fierce drinkers of barbarous life—behold your own!
She danced. This is the night of her ruined girlhood.
She has earned it. She whirls the vesture of saints
For her scarves. The blood has bellowed. That Herodian lust
Burns already in the narrow groin, not long to be slaked.
On a plate, held high, tilted to the arrogant zest of life,
The great face of the innocent rides somberly in,
Black-mouthed, a terrible hole of condemnation cracked in the
    jaw,
Rebuking the confrontation of ecstasy and sin,
The dangerous edge teetering yet in those coinless eyes.
Into these disbelieving hearts, these faithless sallow souls,
The intrepid face thrusts its spleenless accusation, one final time.
Strutting, the outrageous, excessive girl confronts them,
Brandishing into the aghast male faces, flattened on the nexus
Of the opposed female will, her bloody pledge.
"Look!" her exultant eyes, her flaunting, indemnable lips
Exact it. "This is my trophy! I have asked
What none before me has dared! I dance henceforth
In the image of saints! I possess my desire!"

                                        Nobody laughed.
In the choked silence someone kicked a musician, and the zither
Screeched, a shrill hysterical bleat of masculine consternation.
Smoldering, her face flushed with aggression and contempt,
The umbrageous girl flounced menacing out, dragging her prize.
Her mother had won.

                Northward on straw, beside another mountain,
Over against another sea, slept one, the latchet of whose shoe
Even the Baptist faltered to free. His dream dredged deep,
Seeing in time profanations more vile than the prophet's doom
Heaped on the platters of human forbearance.
Let the far tides fall. Let all the world's rivers
Run down to the sea. Jesus dreamed on straw
The inexorable prescience of the lurid fact.

The killed visage, clenched in the hands of the grinning girl,
Stared out the timelessness of the real,
Beholding nothing at all it had not foreseen
Many years back, in the womb, when the weak limbs,
Sphered in those lapsing waters of life, that fertile
Plangent sea, sprang the upsurgent body against those walls
As the truth shocked through, sharp in that trance
As a sent sign; as stones, struck under water,
Pierce to the swooning drowner's ear, rouse him urgently up . . .
So did John joy. In his wild womb-dance
He broke the stupor that obsessed the race,
Ancient of doom, the hauteur of the human province
Clamped like an ice cap on the surd heart;
The thaw of a sublimity that would soon, on his birth,
Unseal forever the sleep-dragged eyes, disburden
The breast of its fierce remorse,
And loose the vein of the tremendous tongue
That would thunder in the Redemption.

II. JUDITH AND HOLOFERNES

Then said Holofernes unto her, "Drink now, and be merry with us."
So Judith said, "I will drink now, my lord, because my life is
magnified in me this day more than all the days since I was born."

—THE BOOK OF JUDITH

Saint Judith crouched. About her loins
The instructed provocation of the harlot's intelligence
Or the widow's pang; the smoldering
Anticipatory inflection, flit nimbus of explicit consent,
Reckless awesomeness of the traducer's perversity
In the discipline of the saint.

Did a demon sodden the conqueror's brain,
Dredged with black wine, or was it an angel?
Holofernes, watching her fool with his cumbrous gear,

Would never know. She dragged the cutlass out of its sheath,
Gravely impressed, mocking over its honed edge,
Her dusked eyes darkening: "When the sword of my lord
Bites blood, in the mad battle, let my hope sing it home . . ."

She toyed with it, binding her scarf on the ponderous hilt
For favor, fondling the pendulous tassels she found there,
Curling finger and thumb round the thirsting point,
A spidery tickle. "Let it bring down the proud,
For which I have come to you, a woman's weakness
In the stitch of God's grace . . ."
She mocked her mouth at him over its edge,
The razor-stroked steel. "When my lord
Has pinked at last his terrible blade
I will quench my desire . . ." The conqueror grinned,
Lolling his muscular hams on their print,
The double indentation of crushed cushions,
Where his strong legs spread, and blinked sidewise.
"Promise," she mocked, "When my lord
Has blooded his terrifying blade, he will not forget
Where he learned his secrets . . ."

                                        Outside in the camp
The cohorts slumped in sleep, collapsed on their weapons.
Above the bed, that deceptive keep of obsidional debauchery,
Where the masterplan of covert assault lay stretched and waiting,
A small lampflame dangerously flirted, sulked on its wick,
Twisting about like a snake's torso flexing to strike.
The great silks of the tent enveloped them,
In the voluminous silence of fortuitous stealth.
The camp lay dead. They alone looked to each other,
Contained in the gaze of engrossed betrayal,
And each banked passion—he, the inveterate rapacity
Of the nerve's conquisitional itch; she, the indominate rigor
Of the martyr's faith, who looks in the lion's distended jaw

And never flinches. For each, obsessedly fixed on the other's eyes,
This instant was all. And they swayed there, like mating snakes,
Loth to dispel it, too wise
In the stratagems of hate and desire
To seize too soon.

                "You understand," she said to him gravely,
"Something of what a woman is, I can see that."
(The light on her loins, the numinous fire
Fluxing out of her breast's slow fall.)
"I am not the first in my lord's life,
Being but a poor latecomer here,
Where others have lain, glad to make of their body a bed
For the chief's ease. Where are they now?
But how could they regret it? Perhaps my lord,
When he gives me leave, will find my gift,
Among his memorable accomplishments, not too
Utterly inconsequential, not too
Tiresomely trite?"

            She stirred, ruthless,
Projecting out of all her surfaces
The tyranny of her truth.

              And the conqueror smiled.
A woman of brains and sensibility, he respected that.
In his cagey respect, rooted down in his being's base,
The seminal propensity engendered in flux
Its thick provocation, the measure of the male.
Let her choose her time, a subtle mind
In a serpentine body, and when she chose it
The time, he knew, would be richer for that.

He drank deep, the aura of suggestibility
And the smoldering anticipation the sense stirs,
When a man expects what he holds already in the seething brain,

Excites the profile of deranged rapture,
Rush and roll of the blood plunged, the explicit
Female debouchment, so long allured and at last relinquished,
And the groin's crude grunt. He smiled, drinking again,
Compulsively, nursing his sodden tactical hunch,
Drinking and waiting, the sovereign passion
Spreading down in his deeps, a sleepy fire.

God uses the devil, Job proved that.
But does the devil use God? Holofernes, headless in hell,
Will twist forever on the demon's nail,
Crucified on the splayed tree of the sexual act,
Ejaculating out of the dismasted shoulders
The orgastic splurge of neuric excess.
Here, in his wantonest moment, the demon within him
Slumbered and slept, drugged down with wine,
Stupefied in the clog of diffused consciousness,
The guzzle of omnivorous thirst.
But the angel that lit her ecstatic face,
Limned with an exquisite ravishment,
Perfecting on the lips and the sinuous body
The delineaments of unspeakable gluttings,
The giddiness of delight in the shamelessness of grace—
That angel creates, and in the discrepant achievement
Outdoes the devil. Holofernes, divided on his own blade,
His swart head slewed back and chopped off,
Hewn loose in two hacks, and the bloated trunk
Stiffening in the cerement of his own arras,
His head balled up, stashed away in a woman's purse,
Never again to gloat in triumph on the proud neck
When battles are joined and maids deflowered,
Sings his own requiem, the terrified bellow
Of distempered blood. Oh, what angel of angels
Steeled the widow's wrist, purged it of weakness,
Hardened the voluptuous forearm for its zigzag crunch,
Endowing in the suave insinuative shoulder

The dint of Samson, and made all muscle the supple stern,
That had promised to tuck like a frisking minx
His wild uncircumcized pang—what angel enveloped her
When she squatted and struck, the cutlass
Slammed down and hacked through, the exposed jugular
Writhing back from the steel, as a garden snake
Frenzies under a woman's hoe
When she hews her greens in the wind-wade of spring—
All about the bull body, sacrificial,
The mithraic cadence of spent libido,
His legs asprawl, and the sprawled sex,
That would never again bleed a virgin's seal,
Dabbed with slick blood . . .

                    O ravishment of God
On the unspeakable face of the transfixed Jewess,
Awesome in its divine righteousness, its terrible truth,
To stand at last, like Salome alone, a man's head
Gripped in her hands!

                    Grieve you warriors!
Mourn your loss you great men of battle,
Blood-drunk dukes of carnivorous life,
Out there on the mesa, asleep on your spears,
Bedeviled by dreams of women and gods!
The moon steals over the stupefied camp, crisply,
And blesses at last the besieged city,
Softening the contours of warfare and weather,
Erasing the scars of violence, hate, the perverse tribulation
Of energic despair, atoning at last
In its delicate presence the harsh male madness
And the spoilage of man. The strange woman
Glides through the camp like a young goddess
Bearing her gifts, back through the thorn
And the desert gravel, over the flints,
Picking her way through camel dung and the urine of mules,

Drifting back to the beleaguered city that gave her birth,
Where the greybeard fathers, impotent,
Sit on their mats, invoking the inscrutable God,
Of whom in fact they have quite despaired,
To make in this hour some bland interpolation,
Discover within their obscure hearts,
Blind with the anxiousness of earth
And the libidinous rage that terrors their days,
The germ of rebirth, purging from their souls
The fraudulent thirst of the sword's conceit,
The furious grudge of His siege.

THE CONVERSION OF SAINT PAUL

And as he went on his journey, it came to pass that he drew nigh to Damascus; and suddenly a light from heaven shined round about him. And falling on the ground, he heard a voice saying to him: "Saul, Saul, why persecutest thou me?" Who said: "Who art thou, Lord?" And he: "I am Jesus whom thou persecutest. It is hard for thee to kick against the goad." And he trembling and astonished, said: "Lord, what wilt thou have me to do?" And the Lord said to him: "Arise . . ."

—THE ACTS OF THE APOSTLES

Jerusalem
Died in the dust.
They took the short route,
Up the river to Hippos,
Then straight through the desert,
Eight days, approaching
At noon the heat-veiled city,
Oasised, green-cool in the desert,
The vernal gleam of an opal.

And coming out of that vastness the noonday sun
Blazed like the wrath of Yahweh, intense righteousness,
The downfalling stroke of noon.
Heat danced the meridian.
Bare ridges, steel blue, those ribbed
Horizon-haunters, swathed in the welter of ripples,
Air tingling, the stretched
Sizzle of hotness.

And the gaunt Pharisee, seeing it, stood in his stirrups.

Damascus, at last before him, the fragrant, plangent city,
Pearl-grey, cinctured about with pomegranates,
The slender stems of its date palms,

Lovely as a girl laughing by well-water,
Slim-vesseled virgin—but tainted, tainted,
Infected in the low place,
Crawling with christ-lovers,
Scabrous infestation . . .

Crash!

A brilliance so bright
The noon blanked black
Overhead where the sun was;
Intense radiance unwombed;
One lasting flash,
One fast unfaceable spasm.

The horse uprearing
Outsprung from under,
Forked ears pronged
On the blinding intenseness,
The high pawed hooves . . .

Crash!

The clang of fallen metal, armor
Rang on the road, the flailed scabbard,
That loose-sprung blade, grit-grating,
Steel on stone.

Dust swallowed him up.

He lay enveloped, as one dead,
Stunned, swathed in dust,
Stupefied . . .

Saul! Saul!

Far off, beyond the Caucasuses, the innominate nightfall
Flows like music on the deepening steppes.
The homesick yak-herder, hunched against fatigue,

Dreams of the skin dusk of his yurt
And the slow hands of his hill wife.
Many the nights, many the nights of the love-rank bed,
And the blind suck of her mouth . . .

But for the Pharisee,
In the bitten dust outside Damascus,
This night is new.
In his light-splintered brain
The local planets of his limited vision
Split and swept out,
Spending their ruin through the titanic vastness.
Shrill specks of consciousness
Crying the railing pang of mortality
They flecked and died out.
In that dream of oblivion
His ears rang with the terror of galactic silence:
The swung span of such lunar darknesses
The world never knows . . .

Saul! Saul!

Music of an exhalation
Softer than the murmur of love-pledges,
More vibrant than woman's wisdom
Or the sudden concourse of tongues,
Slower than the measure of migratory waters,
The lapse of cool oceans,
Or night-risen wind over fern . . .

Saul! Saul!

Sibilant, richer than the labial
Meaning of myth, a muted inflection,
Slower than the filmy lip-suck of waters,
As modulant as waterways
In their slowed convergence,

Through reed shallows,
Where the bulrush staves
Tugged at the tossing ark of Moses,
The dark drift of the Nile . . .

Saul! Saul!
In the red brain of the ruined prophet
The constellated pillars of enforced justice
Crack the hammers of retort and fall still.

He scrabbles his hands.
He claws his fingernails
Crazy in gravel,
His brute-blind, dust-dazed head
Addled in consternation.

He clutches his clothes,
He pants his pain-fed animality,
Ho gasps his moan.

They help him terrified up,
Limp him blind to Damascus,
The blistering heat
Beating him on;
His weak hands wilt,
His sobbing tongue
Blind and babbling,
His feet lurching the dust-blind,
Dog-dunged way.

Behind him the desert
Flattens its immemorial witness,
As sterile and lifeless as the unfructified law,
The terrible tentacular rigidity

Of the scorpion and the crab.
As explicit as the adder and the bat-faced jackal
It flattens its unreflective discipline,
Exacts its will.

And all the chuckholes
Back down the road to Jerusalem,
Tremble in the righteous
Outrage of the sun,
The light-drunken Lord,
Horrified of sin,
Dancing his meridianial
Dance of death,
Down toward darkness,
The rain-wreathed regions of the vaster west,
And the salt suck-down of the sea . . .

It is done. Already the desert
Merges its sweeping affirmation,
Redisposing its deft propinquity,
Counting all interruptions
As accidental as birth and as irrelevant as death.
For all its sovereign imperative
The instant must die.
Even the stallion, shock-stung,
Who, pitching that rider down in the dust,
Roached up and ran, even he
Will only a little longer keep,
Etched on the creases of his brain,
The solar-drenched image that flung him so,
Galvanic, pawing the air,
His shrieked nostrils and his socket-sprung jaw,
Tooth-champing, the girth-bursted saddle
Shook free and flung far,
When he leaped loose, and flank-cowering
Ran like a pelted cat,

Bolted for life like some stoned cur,
To meet his death—even he,
Who etched the graph of its sharp kinetic
On his fine-wrought nerve,
Will not hold it long.

That furious light,
More piercing than the atom's
Convulsive flex, and more terrible
Than the star's expiring orgasm,
Will not subsist in his hollow skull
After he dies, thirst-famished,
Out there under those desert cliffs,
Perched upon by those teetering,
Wind-spermed birds, come balancing down,
Leg-light, on the relinquished carcass,
To pick the eyeball expertly out,
Snake forth the brain,
Gobble the entrail and the succulent gut.
Given the desert's immemorial erasures,
Its bone-clean effacements,
This light will die.

But he who bridled that stallion up
And recklessly spurred him,
Who himself lies now like one murderously mauled,
Flat on a bed in the walled town,
Lugging his slow breath,
The stiff-engined heart
Laboring in the shaken ribs,
In him it subsists,
As carefully seeded as some night-borne coal,
Braved through blizzards to a stone-cold hearth,
Where, breathed into life,
Its ray will kindle a glory up,
Warm a world . . .

Before he dies this lapsing,
Shut-tongued wretch
Will spend that vision on the world's width,
Spell utterly out the supreme implication,
Divest his soul of all that was dealt him,
There in the dust, when he lay listening,
His stupefied mind expanding about that central core,
Grasping its depth of total containment,
Its limitless scope. Blind in his bed,
The stony visage, glacial as the implacable rockfaces
That stare east up to Everest,
Thaws in the flow of an understanding.
Peaceful, touched and atoned,
He sinks into sleep. And the scale
Flakes from his eyes.

IN SAVAGE WASTES

A monk ran into a party of handmaids of the Lord on a certain journey. Seeing them he left the road and gave them a wide berth. But the Abbess said to him: If you were a perfect monk, you would not even have looked close enough to see that we were women.

—VERBA SENIORUM

A hermit who has lived a long time in the desert experiences great dearth of spirit, and one night, exhausted, falls asleep over his prayers. He is awakened by a knock at the door, and opening it beholds two nuns. They explain that they are on pilgrimage and have become separated from their company, and beg of him shelter for the night. He graciously shows them into his cell, and prepares to spend the night outside so that they may have its privacy to themselves. However, once inside they lock the door and throwing off their habits reveal themselves as naked succubi. They cast a spell over him, and seduce him, and there is not a shred of sensory excitation which they do not stimulate within him and gratify.

In the morning the monk wakes up and realizes he has dreamed. There is no sign either of pilgrims or succubi, nor any evidence of the disorders so real to him during the night. The monk leaves his desert cell and begins to make his way back to the world. As he goes he meets a young man, vaguely familiar to him, who is newly dressed in a monk's habit and is entering the desert to become a solitary. The young monk seems to recognize him and calls him by name; kneeling before him he asks his blessing. Then he says to him: "Tell me, Father, what is the greatest blessing and the greatest curse of the spiritual life?" The monk replies: "Sleep. In sleep we dream. In dreams we betray ourselves. In betrayal we discover ourselves. In self discovery we lose our innocence. In loss of innocence we gain knowledge. In knowledge we gain wisdom. In wisdom we recover innocence. God be with you." With these words the monk leaves the young man, whom he now recognizes as himself, and reenters the world.

I too, O God, as you very well know,
Am guilty.

And the desert gorges, those hacked
Untendered waste-worlds of the soul—

What buzzard's eye from its sun-skewered height
Has peered such places,
Pierced such deeps?

The gullies of death, the engorged
Arroyos, badlands of the hackling heart,
The scups of perversity.

I too, I too, as You very well know . . .

Where the kites are shrieking
There reeks the carcass.
Where the treasure is sunk
There cowers the heart.
Having done such things in the green wood
What will I do in the dry?

Guilt-stretched the night.
Choked in the abstract dimension
I see the eyes of my lust.

Have pity on me, have pity on me,
At least you my friends,
For God hath touched me.

For the light is lost.
Great darknesses drop over the waste.
The hostile stars burn green as cat's eyes
In their depth of dread.
There is not an owl on the greasewood,
There is not a saw-whet on the creosote bush
To keep a man company.

I too, O God, as You very well know,
Am guilty.

For I sought and found not,
I searched, but was not successful.
When I failed, You drew back the veil,
And I am in terror.

In terror,
Who gazed in the poisonous pool.
In dread,
Who sucked of its jet.
Am sick and am sick
Who have seen to myself,
Begging forgiveness of my own self,
In what I have done.

For if You, O God, can pardon a man,
Should himself be less merciful?

Let me forgive myself of my terrible sins
That I may have peace.

Let me have mercy on myself
Or I will hang myself on a juniper tree
To wipe out my guilt.

There will be flints and grits forever in my bed.
There will be cinders in my mush.

I am burned black.
I am back from a bitter journey.
I have cruised hell.

Let me forgive myself
That thought to be a saint
And am proved a monster.

That thought to be righteous and good,
And am proved vile.

That thought myself to be the Christ
And am found the Devil.

Windless, the air dead, the night hot.
Can I find, in fact, the friendliness of a human face?

Forgive me, O God, that my heart should hold such horrors.

The vast desert stars.
The waterless ridges.
The vacant gullies.

When I am proved out
I will come back to my people
And confess my crimes.

For I will make friends of the sinner
And comfort him in his plight.
I will pick the evildoer up from the ground
That he may take heart from his evil
And hunger the good.

I will bless the bad,
That he may be brought from madness,
May be made whole.

Speechless the stars.
No word in the wind.
The hell of nature defiled
Shuts her dread face.

For there is no man that is righteous
But carries somewhere in his salty heart
A worse villainy.